Schnauzer

a play in one act

David Yezzi

EXOT BOOKS
2018

EXOT BOOKS
NEW YORK

www.exottreasures.com/exotbooks

Copyright 2018 EXOT BOOKS
All Rights Reserved
Typeset in Trebuchet MS & Times New Roman
ISBN: 978-0-9898984-4-7
Cover & Design: Julio M. Perea

Acknowledgments

The Baltimore Poets' Theatre production of *Schnauzer* opened at Single Carrot Theatre, Baltimore, on February 5, 2016, with the following cast:

Shayla (and Master's Voice) ..... Claire Aniela
Clip (and Lulu) ..... Austin Allen
Pam ..... Julia Friedrich

Direction ..... Tim Freborg
Stage Manager ..... Sophie LaCava
Dramaturge ..... Q-mars Haeri
Designer ..... Michael Vincent

Portions of the play have appeared in *Linebreak* and *Verse Wisconsin*. A version of Shayla's opening monologue appears in *Birds of the Air* (Carnegie Mellon Poetry Series). The author is grateful for production support from the Andrew W. Mellon Foundation and Johns Hopkins University. Special thanks to Jim Milton, Katherine Robinson, Mollie Rotmensch, and Brandon R. Weber for their valuable contributions.

For Issa and Juno

CHARACTERS

Shayla,
20

Clip,
21, then 31, then 33

Pam,
30, then 32

Lulu,
a dog (Clip)

Master's Voice
(Shayla)

SCENES

Scene One:
A college dorm room, early 90s.

Scene Two:
Ten years later. A swimming pool in the suburbs.

Chorus:
A sidewalk.

Scene Three:
Twelve years after scene one. A hospital room.

Scene One

In black, the beeping of a hospital heart monitor. The beeps become the rhythmic barks and yelps of a dog. Then: faraway barking segues into the synthesizer solo from Pink Floyd's "Dogs."

Lights up on a typically untidy New England college dorm room. There is an Eastern hippy-temple feeling to the décor. In bed, twined in a sheet is CLIP, a senior, in white boxers. Kneeling over him, dressed in a t-shirt and shorts, SHAYLA, is sniffing him. He is gagged and tied to the bedposts with rope and handcuffs. After a moment, he wakes up. He writhes and tries to speak.

Shayla

Shh! Stay!
        You're making too much noise.
                Bad boy.
(Whispering.) Think about it . . . What's it gonna look like:
you in my room, on an all-girls floor of the dorm?
I think you'd want to think about that fact.
Look, I'll take that gag off, if you just sit still.

(He moans.)

        You know those cuffs
would hurt a lot less if you'd just relax.
Remember, you're the one who put them on.
You put them on. Then you passed out,
like you were dead. I tried waking you, even
pried your lids up but your eyes were white,
which scared me cause I thought you might be dead.

(She takes a photo of him with a disposable camera that she wears around her neck.)

I've never seen a person so . . . zoned out.
You know, I'm pretty sure you can overdose on Ecstasy.
I think your spine leaks, or something like that.

(Her tongue flops out, and she acts like a corpse, lying against him.)

Sometimes, I try to imagine that I'm dead,
as if I weren't here, as if I was
invisible and I could walk around
with everything still going on like usual.
Without me.
What difference would it make if I were gone?
Zero.

(She wraps a piece of rope around her neck. He struggles nervously.)

>It's okay with me. It's true. But it's nice of you
>to try to disagree.
>>You are such a sweetie.

(She snuggles next to him.)

>I'm always blown away by people's kindness.
>It really knocks me out, you know?
>Those rare times we let down the guard we use
>to keep the freaks away? And, let's face it,
>they're everywhere—the crosstown bus, the bank,
>the grocery store, joggers in Central Park,
>especially them, so smug, so master race.
>That's why I can't believe we ever met.

(He grunts.)

>Not you and me. I mean this guy I loved.
>I didn't really plan it, didn't ask for it,
>you know, and that's how come I knew I loved him.
>I loved him. And I also loved his dog.

(Clip makes a sound like "Huh?")

>*My* dog loved *his* dog. That's the way we met,
>at the dog run . . .

(She takes out a small photo book and shows him pictures.)

>Actually, there were two near me:
>a bigger run—much fancier but farther—
>and, underneath the bridge, a scrappy one.
>I started at the nicer one, you know,
>walked down the extra blocks, because I thought,
>since there were more dogs there, the better chance
>of finding one that Lulu'd want to play with.
>The nicer one had lots of dogs and space.
>But it was crap. The dogs there all were dead.
>I mean they just seemed kind of dazed, like robots,
>as if the life had just drained out of them.
>Meanwhile, the people there—the regulars—

they didn't notice. All they did was talk,
blah-blah-blah, blah-blahbeddy-blah, blah-blah
talking about the way the neighborhood
had gone to hell, how they had grown up there,
about their fancy breeders. Yak-yak-yak.
The dogs were sweet. Mostly they just looked stunned,
since no one played with them or threw a ball.
People would get annoyed when dogs would play,
but that's why the dogs were *there*—to rub and roll
and chase, and hump each other in the dirt.
Lulu they just hated; she loved to run.
She tried to get the other dogs to chase her
by nipping at them; no, it wasn't biting.
Nipping. You'd put your finger in her mouth,
and she'd just hold it there between her teeth,
possess it, so you couldn't take it back,
but never even hurting you, you see?
To them she was a wolf: blood-thirsty, feral,
and everyone would whisper when she came.

Then Lulu got a pigeon. It wasn't her fault.
Lulu was a huntress; she hunted everything,
mice and squirrels, and earthworms she'd dig up.
But what she wanted most of all were pigeons.
She would pounce at them, every muscle
on fire to catch that bird,
and not just catch it, eat it, too.
I've never seen her looking happier
than in that moment, when her choke collar
zipped tight like a big fish taking a hook,
and her leaping at it, airborne, twisting around
to catch it in her teeth.
                              The people freaked.
I started screaming, pulling on the leash,
but she had it in her mouth, between her paws.
When I reached in to free the thing, she growled,
and I came up with bloody hands and wrists.
It wasn't mine. She would never do that.
Not even in the ecstasy of it.
So, that was it for the fancy uptown run.
We wound up at the dingy run last winter,

mostly empty,
where Lulu met Reynaldo, a scruffy schnauzer.
Lulu and Reynaldo. Hmm.
They ran until their tongues flapped down their chins.
Then Rey-Rey's owner started making small talk—
just casual, like news stuff from the paper,
training tricks, dog stories—like you do.
This guy was just so sweet, so totally charming,
and seeing him I got completely happy.

I waited for him on the days he didn't come.
It felt first like a little irritation,
so that I didn't notice it. But then
I actually ached for him when he was gone.
I told myself that Lulu missed Reynaldo,
but then one morning in the freezing rain
I saw him as we were coming along the river
towards the run, and Lulu started pulling
on her choke chain—she nearly pulled my arm off.
For two whole blocks she strained, just acting nuts.
She pulled the leash free of my hand and ran.
And as I stood there in the sleet I knew
that I had missed him so incredibly
I almost started crying. And the dogs
leapt up to catch each other in their paws,
like ballroom dancers circling the floor,
upright, on hind legs, balanced arm in arm.
I felt like that was us, but not imagined it,
actually felt—as we stood there silently,
unmoving, watching, side-by-side—
that we were pressing up against each other,
swaying into the matted whorls of fur,
my teeth clamped on his skin, saliva flying.
Sometimes I wonder if it isn't possible
that the loves we have in our minds are
the ones that matter to us most of all,
the ones that we take with us to the grave.
I guess I'm sorry that it wasn't him
I was supposed to love. So, now I guess
it's not going to be you either, huh?

(Pause.)

> I'm going to take these off, but understand
> that once you leave this room you won't say anything.
> Unless you want your father and the cops
> to see these pictures.
> I'm not sure how you're going to explain them.

(She sniffs him. He exclaims though his gag. She takes off the cuffs. CLIP removes his gag.)

Clip

What are you doing?!

Shayla

Sniffing?

Clip

You're sniffing me?

Shayla

Awww. Grrrufff. Okay, take it easy big dog.

Clip

(He looks around excitedly, pulls the twisted sheets around him.)

> What time is it?

Shayla

It's noon.
        Graduation Day plus one.
You graduated. Remember. Big day.
Congratulations, senior. You are free.

Clip

(Confused.)

Today is . . . ?

Shayla

        Thursday. Oh, my god.
You should really look into this substance thing.

Clip

(Slowly processing, then somewhat relieved.)

Thursday. Yeah. Okay . . . ah, yeah . . . Okay . . . Okay . . . Shit. Ow. Why was I tied up? You fucking tied me up!

Shayla

        I tied you up?
No, no, no, no, no.
I told you: you tied you up. Your idea.

Clip

(His wrists are sore.)

Damn. Huh.
Look. I'm sorry,
ya know, if things got out of hand last night.
Are we cool?

Shayla

You really don't remember anything, do you?

Clip

No, no, I do. It's coming back. Look, I should probably . . .

Shayla

(Abruptly, angrily.)

Fuck you. Oh, sure. Yeah.

Clip

What?

Shayla

You . . . Yes, you should! What you just said.
You should just . . . go! You're disgusting. I hate you!

Clip

I didn't say that. That's not what I said.

Shayla

So what? So you should probably, *what*?
Stay? Campus security has already been notified.

Clip

Awwwww, shit. *Shit*.

Shayla

Jesus Christ, I'm just kidding.

Clip

No, no, it's not that. Shit.
I think I was supposed to meet my folks somewhere.
Have you seen my phone?

(He looks around.)

Do you know where my shoes are?

Shayla

Where did you see them last?

Clip

(He tries to remember.)

Oh, god. I was freaking drunk.

Shayla

>And then we did X.

Clip

We did Ecstasy? You mean from the bag I had?

Shayla

Uh-huh. We maybe might have done it all.

Clip

What!?

Shayla

I think you got a lot of people high last night.

Clip

Oh, shit. Are you shitting me? That's bad.

(Shayla takes a picture.)

>Stop doing that.

Shayla

>So go.

You can leave, you know. You have free will.
No one's handcuffed you to the bed!

Clip

Oh, I am going. I am gone. I'm out.
I'm sorry but I still don't have my shoes!

Shayla

Well, I didn't fucking take them. I'm not some psycho.
I'm sorry if I threatened you before. It was a joke!
Your secret's safe.
At least until you try to explain this . . .

(She snaps a photo.)

Clip

(He starts rifling through the clothes on the ground and under the bed, occasionally finding something of his own.)

Why are you taking pictures?

Shayla

I'm going to keep them. But don't worry.
They're just for me.
You are freaking cute.
I know I said I wasn't into you,
but I am. I really am.

Clip

Do you always torture guys you party with?

Shayla

Yeah. *(She laughs.)* Sort of. But you can trust me, baby.

Clip

Oh, I'm supposed to trust you? Cause you're so discrete and normal.

Shayla

Forget normal. I think you should kiss me.

(She pulls him to the bed and rolls on top of him.)

Clip

Please get off of me.
I can't breathe . . . I can't breathe.

Shayla

All right! God, you're such a baby.
I'm tired of looking at you. Here's a tip
for your future disastrous relations with women:
leave before they have to kick you out.
Guys like you always overstay their welcome.

Clip

Okay, I'm going! Christ.
Up to five minutes ago I was chained to a bed,
so leaving wasn't really an option.

(She is standing in front of the door.)

Shayla

You're such a little puppy dog.
Why did you come to my room last night?
Why did you follow me home, little puppy?

Clip

Fuck if I know.
Oh god, you know . . . And now I guess
there's no way to just pretend this never happened.

(He closes his eyes.)

No, this definitely happened.

(He attempts a laugh.)

Shayla

No, seriously. Why did you? I'm curious.

(Puzzling it out with difficulty.)

Clip

Because I guess I thought that you were cute.

Shayla

And?

Clip

And what?

Shayla

And what else?

Clip

And because . . .

Shayla

And because you liked the fact I liked you.
That's the way guys work.
There just like little puppies at the pound,
scratching at the glass for someone to pick them.
That's gonna be the key to your whole life.
You'll wind up with the first woman who shows
the least bit of interest in you.

Clip

Fine. So,
I liked you because we were having a good time.

Shayla

And because I put your hand under my shirt.

Clip

Um, yeah. It's possible.
Look, I really do like you.
But I've got to meet my parents now for lunch.

Shayla

Will you be moving back with mom and dad,
while you *sort things out*?
See where you fit in this nihilist, corporate hell
we call our little corner of the globe?

Clip

I'm moving to New York.

Shayla

The Big Apple.
Will you be entering the workforce?

Clip

Yep. I guess so. I'll probably get a temp job,
or something.

Shayla

       God, you're so ambitious.
You trust-fund kids are all alike . . .
Go suffer among the working classes while daddy
shells out for your apartment and your clothes.

Clip

Jealous? Look, I don't want their help. I'm broke.
I honestly don't have a hundred bucks
to my name right now. I'm staying with a guy
I know until I get a job.
No family ties. I don't like to be tied down.

Shayla

Really, I thought you actually kind of enjoyed it.
So what do you want, Clip?

Clip

What do you mean, What do I want? Ha!
Oh, Christ. Is this my exit interview?
I thought I missed it? Very clever how they do this,
drug you at a party, tie you up,
then ask you what your plans are for the future.
Well, let's see. Miss?

Shayla

My name is Shayla.

Clip

I know that. (*He didn't.*) Well, Shayla.
I've decided to put my literature degree to use
saving the human race.

Shayla

People like you don't save the world; they run it.
Isn't that what they told you at Choate,
or wherever you spent your pimply adolescence.
Isn't that where you got the name, Clip?
What is that?

Clip

It's short for Clipper. My real name is Clayton.

Shayla

Is your father a big sailor or something, Clipper?
Big Patrick O'Brien fan?

Clip

They call me Clip because I ruined our couch.
When I was a kid I was kind of a neat freak;
anything slightly messy drove me crazy,
every rough edge or hair left out of place.
I use to get black dirt under my nails
from playing in the yard, fingers and toes
black with heavy crescents of oily dirt,
so disgusting. It used to make me sick.
So I cut my toenails and my fingernails
right down to the skin till they were smooth,
till I couldn't feel the edge of them at all,
except I cut too close and I started bleeding
all over my Mom's white sofa, which I tried to clean,
but the water on it only stained it worse—
silk, I guess. So then they called me Clip.

Shayla

They named you for a childhood pathology?

Clip

Something like that. Know what I want?
I'm going to get as far away as possible
from everything in my life up till now,
their schedule, their rules, my father's business.
Oh, my god, I so don't want to work for my old man.
That's my idea of death. I'll never do it.
Maybe that's why I'm here instead of meeting them.

Shayla

You're a free little birdie. Tweet-tweet, little birdy,
flying over the big city, never touching down.
Except to fall back on those family ties,
when you see the first sign of trouble making rent.
Why build a nest when you can have an aviary?

Clip

Yeah, okay. I gotta go.

Shayla

I know. You said. You want your freedom back.
Off the leash. You don't want to be bound up
anymore. Here's your tie.

(He takes it, and she pulls him toward her.)

Clip

Let go. It's going to tear.

Shayla

But what about me? You can't get rid of me.

Clip

Oh, really.

Shayla

Nope. I'm going to stay with you for a long time.
You're going to think of me every day,
from now on, probably forever.

Clip

Well, that's a mighty long time.
Maybe you could visit me.

Shayla

Maybe I will. You know my mom lives in New York.
We could get a beer.

Clip

You promise?

Shayla

Sure.

Clip

You know, you're actually pretty cool,
when you're not being a psycho.
I don't want you to get the wrong impression.
I don't usually ...

Shayla

Oh, you mean you're not really a scary predator?

(She kisses his neck.)

Clip

Well, it's . . .

Shayla

Or are you just the prey?

(She kisses him on the mouth and continues to kiss and bite his neck.)

Clip

Maybe I should put the cuffs back on.

Shayla

(Grabbing him by the shirt.)

>No, baby.
>I want you to be able to use your hands.

(She growls; he growls back. Blackout. During the scene change we hear "Happy," by The Rolling Stones.)

Scene Two

Sound of a neighbor's dog barking. Water sound. Lights up on the swimming pool of a weekend house in the country. The bed from Scene One is now a lounge chair draped with a beach towel. CLIP in shorts and sunglasses dozes with a magazine across his chest. He is listening to music through headphones and, in his conscious moments, sipping a gin and tonic through a straw. PAM, downstage, in a bathing suit and terrycloth robe is skimming the pool. Light reflects off the water onto her legs. After a moment . . .

Pam

I am so . . . O, just so, so, so, so . . . *(She shudders.)*
God . . . What is wrong with me? I'm such a baby.
Can you even hear me with those things on?
Oh, my god. What is that? Clip,
there's something on the bottom of the pool.
Some kind of animal, I think.
Is that a mole or something? Clip, what is that thing?
Clip? Oh, well. Never mind.

(Still no response, then loudly . . .)

What are you listening to?

(His eyes open. She waves. He removes his earphones.)

Are you listening to something good?

Clip

(Testily.) Nothing. It's just . . . The Stones.
I'm listening to The Rolling Stones, okay?

Pam

Which one?

Clip

Which what?

Pam

Which album are you listening to?

Clip

(Exhaling loudly.) Exile, all right? *On Main Street*?
I'm listening to Keith Richards sing a song
called "Happy," okay!? You happy?

(He stares at her. A pause. She goes back to skimming, then . . .)

Pam

Okay. Just asking.
Exile on Main Street. Is that your favorite?

Clip

Ah, mmm-hmm. Look, I'm listening. Okay? I'm listening!

(He holds up his iPod.)

Pam

Okay! Jeez.

(He shakes his head and puts his headphones back on. Pause.)

(In a deep voice.) "Yes, Pam. *Exile* is a critical favorite
of The Rolling Stones, the culmination of
their classic period in the early 70s.
I particularly admire Keith Richards' vocals
on this one, though some think he sounds too raw.
It's really just a matter of taste." And I
do have good taste. In music. You *(she mouths)* asshole.
That's one of the things you don't know about me.
Or maybe you do. Do you?

(A pause. Then, blithely . . .)

> Always the clever conversationalist.
> It's okay, just ignore me. It's fine with me.
> Cause I don't need to talk to anyone—
> except maybe to a shrink *(laughs)*; that would be nice.
> I mean, I used to need it, need to talk.
> Talk to people. Talk to other people.
> But not anymore. I gave it up. It gave
> me up, I guess, might be the way to put it.
> Oh god, not you. I don't mean that you did,
> not you all by yourself, in isolation.
> But everyone. And sometimes I go days
> without talking to another living soul.
> Well, pleasantries. Like "Have a nice day, Clayton."
> Or "Could you drop my dress off at the cleaners?"
> Or: "There's something dead at the bottom of the pool."
> But that's to you. I don't mean you, exclusively.
> If I go out, like to the grocery store,
> I maybe, if I see my friends, say, "Hi,"
> like to a neighbor or the grocery guy.

(Barking in the distance.)

> Hear that? Whose dog is that?
> That dog's been getting bolder every morning.
> He was over here. Did you see him, Clip?
> Just standing in the middle of the yard.
> He didn't move, just stood there like a statue.
> He had one of those painful looking penises.
> Why do their penises get so red like that?
> Like bloody. Maybe we should get a dog.
> Ruff. Ruff. Ruff. Ruff.

(More barking. She turns to him, pleased. His eyes open.)

> Do you hear that?

Clip

> Are you talking to me?

(PAM laughs, and, seeing that he is still wearing his headphones, she shakes her head and waves him off.)

Pam

Well, that would solve the problem, a nice dog,
a little fur-ball drooling on the bed?
Its little food bowl waiting in the kitchen,
its tail wagging to take it out for a pee?
Sweet little poochie. I'm not sure, though.
That's a lot of responsibility to have
for a creature that leaves messes on the rug.
Rrruff. *(She barks suddenly, then smiles at herself.)*

(A pause. She skims. He swats at a black fly. She sings, distractedly.)

I need a love to keep me happy.
I need a love to keep me happy.
Baby. Baby, keep me happy.
Baby. Baby, keep me happy.

Did you just love the water, when you were little?
We used to spend whole summers by the pool.
I'd stay in till my lips turned almost blue.
As soon as school was out, I'd want to swim,
but it was still too cold in June. We had a rule,
my mother had this rule: it had to be
seventy-five degrees before she'd take us,
before we could even go it had to be
seventy-five, not seventy-three or -four.
The problem is we didn't have a thermometer,
so we'd have to check the temperature by phone.
We'd call in once a minute just to see
if it had gotten warmer. On the phone.
Remember when you could do that? Clayton? Clip?

Clip

What?

Pam

Remember when there was a number you could call
to check the temperature?

Clip

You want to know the temperature?
It's seventy-five degrees.

(Pause.)

Pam

> Oh. I should go swimming.

Clip

Not me. Too freaking cold. It's freezing out here.
I feel like it's wintertime all over again.

Pam

Hey, Clip, I want to tell you something.

Clip

> What?

Pam

Yesterday I saw this crazy thing.
I was sitting by the park, last night, you know,
just people-watching, on a bench—it's dusk—

when this little kid goes by, this boy. He's three
or four, just sitting in his father's arms.
And he's saying to his father, loud enough
so everyone can hear, "I'll burn it down.
I'm going to burn it down! If we go home,
I'm going to burn it down." And the poor father
is all tense, trying not to let it get to him.
Can you imagine?
The kid was talking about his own apartment!
I mean, I can imagine. I think I know
just how he feels. But, of course, he doesn't know
what he's saying. I'm not saying that I want
to burn down the house. Hahahaha!
No, he just knows that he is really mad.
And the father knows he isn't really mad;
he's hungry because he hasn't eaten anything,
or sick or tired or up late past his bedtime.
He's screaming, but it's really something else
that's bothering him, whatever it is, probably nothing.
But what?, I kept wondering. What's bothering you?
What's bothering that little man? That boy.

(CLIP has put his headphones back on.)

I need to tell you something:
I'm leaving you. I've decided I have to leave.

(He doesn't hear her. She goes over to him and sits down.)

Can you stop listening for a minute, Clip?
I need to tell you something. Can you listen
for just a minute? Just only for a second.

Clip

Okay. I'm listening.

Pam

I think that you and I should . . .
I think I may be having a nervous breakdown.

Clip

What? Why do you say that?

Pam

I'm not kidding. I think I might be crazy.

Clip

I think you're just a little stressed right now.
Have a drink or take a nap or . . . swim.
You know, just take a swim. You're all wound up.

Pam

Listen: last week I went completely berserk.
I mean I lost my head, completely lost it.
I was walking by the corner of Lexington Avenue
with a bag from the liquor store, red wine.
It's hot, I think that's part of it, it's hot,
and humid like it was all week last week.
I'm walking in the crosswalk, halfway there,
but the light turns green before I get across.
I'm so completely almost to the curb,
still walking in the crosswalk. So this guy
comes speeding up to me . . .

Clip

>The light was green?

Pam

Yes, the light was green. His light was green.
So what? So what is that supposed to mean?

Clip

Nothing. Nothing. God. It's just a question.
I'm trying to understand the situation.
So the light goes green, and he starts going.

Pam

But just green, just then green. It just turned green
and he starts moving, speeds up, because he sees me.
That's the thing I'm trying to tell you, he
steps on the gas because he sees me there.
And so I stop.
I see him, so I stop right where I am.

Clip

So did he stop?

Pam

Yes, he stopped. You're so goddamned right he stopped.
About an inch away from me. So then,
I lost it. I . . . I . . .

Clip

Jesus, Pammy. So what the hell did you do?

Pam

I don't know. I think I went too far.
It pretty much got out of hand from there.

Clip

So, tell me what happened.

Pam

So he gets out. He gets out of the car.
And he sort of hits me, pushes me like, but with the door.
It's like the door swings and it pushes me, you know?
And the wine bottle breaks on the ground,
which becomes this big red stain like blood.
So I grab him as he's getting out, I grab
his t-shirt, or I guess maybe his arm,
because he starts yelling that I scratched him.
But I swear I didn't, not that I remember.
Then he grabs me with his arm and holds me.
So . . .

Clip

So?

Pam

So, I bit him.

Clip

You bit him?

Pam

(Laughs.) Yes, I bit him.
I know because I felt him in my mouth.
Oh, my god I loved it.
I felt his skin for a second between my teeth.
And then I ran. His blood was in my mouth,
like metal.
And I growled at him: *Grrrrrrrrrrrr.*
"You're crazy lady, you are freaking crazy,"
he yells at me, and in my mind he's right.
I'm crazy. I think I've lost my freaking mind.
I'm standing in the middle of the street,
screaming like a total psychopath,
like it's a crime scene or an accident or something.
And you know what? I couldn't give a shit.
I just watched it happen, just like on TV.
Like on a cop show, when people act like that.

Clip

Pam, you gotta relax . . .

Pam

Relax? Don't freaking tell me to relax!
(Laughs.) I mean, you're right. I do need to relax.
I'm going crazy. Am I completely crazed?

Clip

He revs his car at people in the street.

He should lose his license. What did the cops say?

Pam

They never came. I don't think he ever called them.

Clip

That's because he knew that he was wrong.

Pam

So I was right. So fine. So fucking what?
What does my being right entitle me to?
Justice? Human decency? Respect?
It doesn't work that way. There is no right.
You can do everything exactly by the book.
But that's not enough.

Clip

What's not enough?!?!

Pam

Never mind. I'm sorry. Look, I'm tired.
Go back to listening. I'm okay now.

Clip

Okay. Forget that guy. It's not your fault.

Pam

How is it everything makes sense to you?
Does nothing ever not make sense to you?
Everything's on track.
That's your gift, your blessing, if you will.
It's all been laid out for you. It all makes sense.
Prep school, college, working with your dad.
Every edge is smooth. So, good for you.
You know what? Good for you.

Clip

Fuck you, Pam. You know, you . . . Arghhhhhh!
Hahahahahahahahahahaha!
You have no idea. I mean . . .
You are so completely out of touch with everything,
you're unbelievable . . .
You're in this fucking Cloud Cuckoo Land!

(He calls toward the neighbor's yard.)

Will you please make that dog stop barking!

Pam

Jesus, Clip.

Clip

Look, I'm sorry that you are having a hard time.
Maybe that's my fault. I'm sure as far as you're
concerned, it is. Okay, that's fine. It's all my fault.
But I don't see how everything is your problem?

Pam

What do you mean?

Clip

So you're the one who gets to be the crazy one?
You're the one who gets to be upset,
because somehow you think the world has wronged you,
that somehow you didn't get what you signed on for?
I know what you want, but there's nothing I can do about it.
Maybe I'm the one that wants to go a little crazy
for a change!

Pam

I'm sorry.
So, it's my fault? So was it my fault the other day?

Clip

Getting what you want isn't what it's cracked up to be.
Take it from me: life has denied me nothing—
as you never ever tire of reminding me—
and, let me tell you, it is excruciating.
And the worst part is, the very worst part is
I have absolutely no right to be unhappy.
I'm like that fucking dog,
barking all day and pulling at my chain.
I'm going to go tell that guy to shut that dog up.

Pam

Wait. Clip. Clip.

Clip

I'm going back tonight. I'm getting the train.

Pam

Okay. I'll drop you.
Don't go next door. You'll only make it worse.

Clip

Fine.

(CLIP heads toward the house. A pause. She hums.)

> *I need a love to keep me happy.*
> *Baby. Baby, keep me happy.*
> *Baby, Baby . . .*

(She is crying.)

God, I'm such a baby.

(Dog barks.)

> Oh, this is stupid. Maybe I'll get a dog.
> Look: the sun is shining, the temperature
> is a lovely seventy-five degrees.

(Laughs, dips a toe in.)

I should go for a swim.

(Looking into the water, she shivers.)

What is that thing on the bottom of the pool?

(She lowers the skimmer into the pool.)

Come here you poor creature.
Oh, my god. It looks like a little puppy or something.
Come here, baby. Come here, poor baby.

(Sounds of barking nearby. Fade out.)

Chorus

At lights up, LULU bounds on stage on all fours at the end of a long lead that is attached to a collar at her neck.

Lulu

> What is it? What is it?
> What is it? What is it?
> Candy wrapper.
> *Chain. Chain.*
> Cigarette butt. Cigarette butt.
> French fry!
> *Chain. Chain.*

(LULU sniffs the foot of the bench.)

> Who is that? Who is that?
> Who is that? Who is that?
> Little dog? Little dog.
> Bite. Bite little dog.
> *Sniff. Sniff.*
> Pizza crust. Pizza crust.
> *Chain. Chain.*
> *Sniff.*

(LULU's ears perk up. She snaps to attention, surveying the branches above.)

> *Sniff. Sniff.* Pigeon.
> *Sniff. Sniff.* Pigeon.
> *Sniff. Sniff.* Pigeon.
> *Sniff. Sniff.* Eat pigeon.
> *Sniff. Sniff.* Eat pigeon.
> *Sniff. Sniff.* Eat pigeon.

(LULU lunges in the direction of her prey. A voice—SHAYLA's—calls from offstage.)

Voice

LULU, HEEL!

(A jerk on the lead. LULU whimpers slightly.)

Lulu

Chain. Chain.

(Sounds, like barking . . .)

Fuck. Fuck. Fuck.
Fuck. Fuck. Fuck.
Fuck. Fuck. Fuck.
Fuck. Fuck. Fuck.

(LULU snaps to attention, then, straining at the leash . . .)

Sniff. Sniff. Squirrel.
Sniff. Sniff. Squirrel.
Sniff. Sniff. Squirrel.
Sniff. Sniff. Chase squirrel.
Sniff. Sniff. Chase squirrel.

Voice

Lulu, HEEL!

Lulu

(LULU whimpers slightly, then . . .)

Chain. Chain.
Fuck. Fuck. Fuck.
Fuck. Fuck. Fuck.

(LULU yanks the lead and then realizes that she's free.)

Voice

LULU!

(LULU runs off stage barking.)

LULU! NO!

(The sound of a skid and a yelp. Blackout.)

Scene Three

In black, a beeping monitor. Lights up on a hospital room. CLIP lies in bed, unconscious. Beside him, PAM asleep in a chair. SHAYLA enters, wearing a nurse's scrubs. CLIP begins coughing and comes to. He removes his oxygen tube.

Shayla

Shh. It's okay. You're in the hospital.

Clip

I don't remember . . .

(Still waking up.)

Shayla

Everything's fine.

Clip

Pam?

Shayla

She's right here. She's been here the whole time.

Clip

How long . . . ?

Shayla

You've been unconscious.

Clip

She's here?

Shayla

She has been, yes. Are you hungry?

Clip

No, thanks.
What are you doing here? Are you . . . a nurse?

Shayla

I'm not.

Clip

Not?

Shayla

Not here. *You* are here.

Clip

I was thinking about you . . .

Shayla

What were you thinking about?

Clip

I love that smell.

Shayla

You were trying to get away, weren't you?
I can't let that happen. Of course, that's up to you.

(She sniffs him.)

Do you remember that? Sure you do. *(Laughs.)*
You're a sweetie.
Well, I'm still here. That's funny isn't it?

Clip

Yes. It's definitely . . . odd.

Shayla

You're just like a little puppy dog.

Clip

Oh, god. You and the dogs.

Shayla

You think you're any different?

Clip

I don't understand what's going on?

Shayla

What do you want to know: if you're going to wake up?

Clip

Am I not awake?

Shayla

No.
Not sure you're ever going to be?

(She places a pillow over his face. He cries out, until eventually she stops.)

Clip

Get off me. Stop.

Shayla

                                        Oh, buck up, Clip.
Isn't that what you wanted?

Clip

I'm going to ring for the nurse.

(He reaches for the call button.)

Shayla

It's okay, Clayton. You're not, you know.

Clip

Not what?

(She takes his blood pressure.)

Shayla

Dying.

Clip

I'm not?

Shayla

You don't look so good.
And you are unconscious.
But I think that you are going to make it.
I'm sorry if I scared you for a second.

Clip

Why are you here?

Shayla

Why do you think?
Do you not want me here?

Clip

No. Stay.

Shayla

Poor Clipper, always scared of being alone.
But you're not, you see, and that's the irony.

Clip

Why is she here? She's not . . . We're not together.

Shayla

Hm. I'll tell you why . . .
Remember my dog, Lulu.

Clip

Oh, no, look . . .

Shayla

(Strongly.) Staaaay!

Clip

Okay. Fine.

Shayla

What I didn't tell you is that
a few weeks before I met you
Lu ran off, got off the leash.
She ran away in the middle of the city.

Clip

I like your stories. They're always very . . . soothing.

Shayla

Just relax.
This had happened before a few times, not as bad:
we'd be visiting in the country and she'd take off
and I wouldn't worry since there was no road,
no traffic save for the occasional
station wagon or people who'd gotten lost.
And like I said, she always knew her way back.
But this time it was in the city,
out on Second Ave. And *bang*! She was gone.
It wasn't her fault. She couldn't help herself.
I guess she must have seen something—
a pigeon or a squirrel—and she jerked loose
of her collar and ran off down the block.
Then, she looked back,
looked right at me and saw me standing there.
And she realized just then that she was free,
that I no longer had a hold of her.
So, she took off around the next corner.
And I waited for the screech,
the sound of horns and the crash. And when I got
to the next corner and looked Lulu was gone.

Clip

That's terrible.

Shayla

And after about an hour of wandering around
I gave up hope.
I was cold and embarrassed and scared.

And I couldn't stand the thought of coming across her
run over, or maimed, or who knows what.
I got angry, at myself. I blamed myself,
but I blamed Lulu mostly for her nature,
something in her blood that got her killed,
that finally did her in, so not my fault.

Clip

It's not your fault.

Shayla

See, that's what happens when someone is dying:
we look away.
They found her floating in the river: drowned.

Clip

Why are you telling me this?

Shayla

How many visitors do you think you've had
since you've been in a coma—oh, sure,
a handful maybe when you first came in—
but how many since someone turned off the lights?
No one. Just her. And you still don't know why.

Clip

No, I don't.

Shayla

What happens to a person when they die,
do you know? And don't look at me,
I don't know either. I'm no freaking angel.

Clip

I never would have taken you for one.

Shayla

Thank you. Cause I'm not your friend, you know.
Interesting what gets lodged way down
in that little brain of yours.
Pam, on the other hand, is here. And now I'll tell you why.
Sometimes after people look away, they look back.
So here she is.
She stays here night and day hoping you'll wake up.

Clip

What if I don't want to wake up?
Everything's so messed up, you know?
How did that happen?
It's like there's this soundtrack in my head
but it's different from what's really going on.
So, I just turn it louder.
Other people hear it all the time:
the music of what's really going on.
But not me.
Lying here it's not life I miss.
I miss taking life for granted,
the way kids do. The way we did.
I drove that car off the road on purpose.
No. It was an accident,
but I was heading for that. Just a matter of time.

(He's out of breath. She replaces his oxygen tube, kisses his forehead.)

Shayla

Hmm. Bye.

Clip

When is she going to wake up?

Shayla

That's not the question.

Clip

What is the question?

Shayla

The question is: when are you?

(Pause.)

Clip

And what about you?

Shayla

Me? I'm barely here. I'm not here at all.

Clip

I want to go back.

Shayla

I can't help you with that.

Clip

I can't breathe. Hold on to me.

Shayla

She's right there.
You've only got a minute.

Clip

My lungs are full of water.
Why won't you help me?

Shayla

Bye, Clayton.

(He pulls the tube out and begins gasping for breath. Pam wakes up.)

Clip

Can't breathe.

(His choking and coughing sounds like barking . . .)

Pam

Clayton. Oh, god. Nurse. Nurse!

(She presses the oxygen tube to his nose.)

Oh, thank God. Clayton, breathe!
He's awake! He's Awake!

(Blackout.)

CURTAIN

About the Author

David Yezzi's latest books of poetry are *Birds of the Air* and *Black Sea*. A former director of the Unterberg Poetry Center of the 92nd Street Y, he teaches in the Writing Seminars at Johns Hopkins and edits *The Hopkins Review*. Yezzi was a founding member of San Francisco's Thick Description theater company, and his verse plays *On the Rocks* and *Dirty Dan & Other Travesties* have been performed in New York and regionally. His libretto for David Conte's opera *Firebird Motel* was issued on CD by Arsis. As an actor, he has appeared in plays by Brecht, Shakespeare, Shaw, and Goethe, both in the United States and Europe.

OTHER TITLES AVAILABLE FROM EXOT BOOKS

Veil On, Veil Off, John Marcus Powell ~ 2018
A Special Education, Meredith Bergmann ~ 2014
Glorious Babe, John Marcus Powell ~ 2014
Questions, Richard Loranger/Bill Mercer ~ 2013
Turn, Ann Drysdale ~ 2013
Tomorrow & Tomorrow, David Yezzi ~ 2013
Facing The Remains, Tom Merrill ~ 2012
Blue Wins Forever, Paco Brown ~ 2012
They Can Keep The Cinderblock, Mike Lane ~ 2012
Colors, Jay Chollick ~ 2011
Loony Lovers, John Marcus Powell ~ 2011
Filled With Breath: 30 Sonnets by 30 Poets, ed. Mary Meriam ~ 2010
Let Me Be Like Glass, Adriana Scopino ~ 2010
What's That Supposed To Mean, Wendy Videlock ~ 2010
We Internet In Different Voices, Mike Alexander ~ 2009
11 Films, Jane Ormerod ~ 2008
Aquinas Flinched, Rick Mullin ~ 2008
Graceways, Austin MacRae ~ 2008
Prospero At Breakfast, Alan Wickes ~ 2008
Sometime Before The Bell, Ray Pospisil ~ 2006
The Countess Of Flatbroke, Mary Meriam ~ 2006
Blue Glass Cities, Mark Allinson ~ 2006
Prolegomena To An Essay On Satire, R. Nemo Hill ~2006
William Montgomery, Quincy R. Lehr ~ 2006

ORDER ONLINE AT ~www.exottreasures.com/exotbooks

www.ingramcontent.com/pod-product-compliance
Lightning Source LLC
Chambersburg PA
CBHW070439010526
44118CB00014B/2106